Shadow Magic

SHADOW MAGIC

By Seymour Simon

Illustrated by Stella Ormai

Lothrop,
Lee & Shepard Books
New York

LIBRARY OF CONGRESS CATALOGING IN PUBLICATION DATA
Simon, Seymour.   Shadow magic.   Summary: Explains
what shadows are and how they are formed, and tells how
to make a sundial and a shadow show.   1. Shades and
shadows—Juvenile literature. 2. Sundials—Juvenile
literature.   [1. Shadows. 2. Shadow pictures. 3. Sundials.
4. Amusements] I. Ormai, Stella, ill.
II. Title.   QC381.6.S56   1984   535'.4   84-4433
ISBN 0-688-02681-8   ISBN 0-688-02682-6 (lib. bdg.)

Look around on a bright, sunny day.

Wherever the sun shines, things are in the light.

But there are lots of dark spots too.

We call the dark spots shadows.

Look at your shadow.

When the sun shines on one side of you,

your shadow is on the other side.

When you walk, your shadow walks.

When you run, your shadow runs.
When you stop, your shadow stops.
Wave your hands, and jump up and down.
What does your shadow do?

What makes a shadow?
Hold a rock, a leaf, and this book
in the sunlight.
You can't see through these things,
and the sunlight does not shine through them.
They make dark shadows.

Hold a piece of tissue paper or waxed paper
in the sunlight.
You can't see through these things very well,
but a little bit of sunlight shines through them.
They make lighter shadows.

WAXED PAPER   TISSUE PAPE

Hold some plastic wrap or a piece of cellophane
in the sunlight.
You can see through these things,
and most of the sunlight shines through them.
They make almost no shadows at all.

CELLOPHANE

Now can you tell what shadows are?
Shadows are dark spots made by things
that do not let sunlight through.
Lampposts and trees make shadows.
Buildings and umbrellas make shadows.
Cars and bicycles make shadows.
Cats and dogs make shadows.
Birds on the wing and airplanes high in the sky
make shadows too. But you must look quickly
to see them.

Sometimes a cloud crosses in front of the sun.
It makes a big shadow on the ground.
The ground becomes darker.
When the cloud moves away,
the sun shines on the ground again,
and the shadow is gone.

Have you ever seen cloud shadows moving
across a field or a street?
They glide silently along,
covering the ground with a blanket of darkness.
When clouds fill the sky,
they hide the sun.
Their shadows make the day dark and gray.

Planet Earth has a shadow too.
The sun shines on one side of Earth.
It is day on that side of our planet.
The other side of Earth is in shadow.
It is night in Earth's shadow.
Night follows day and day follows night
as our planet turns.

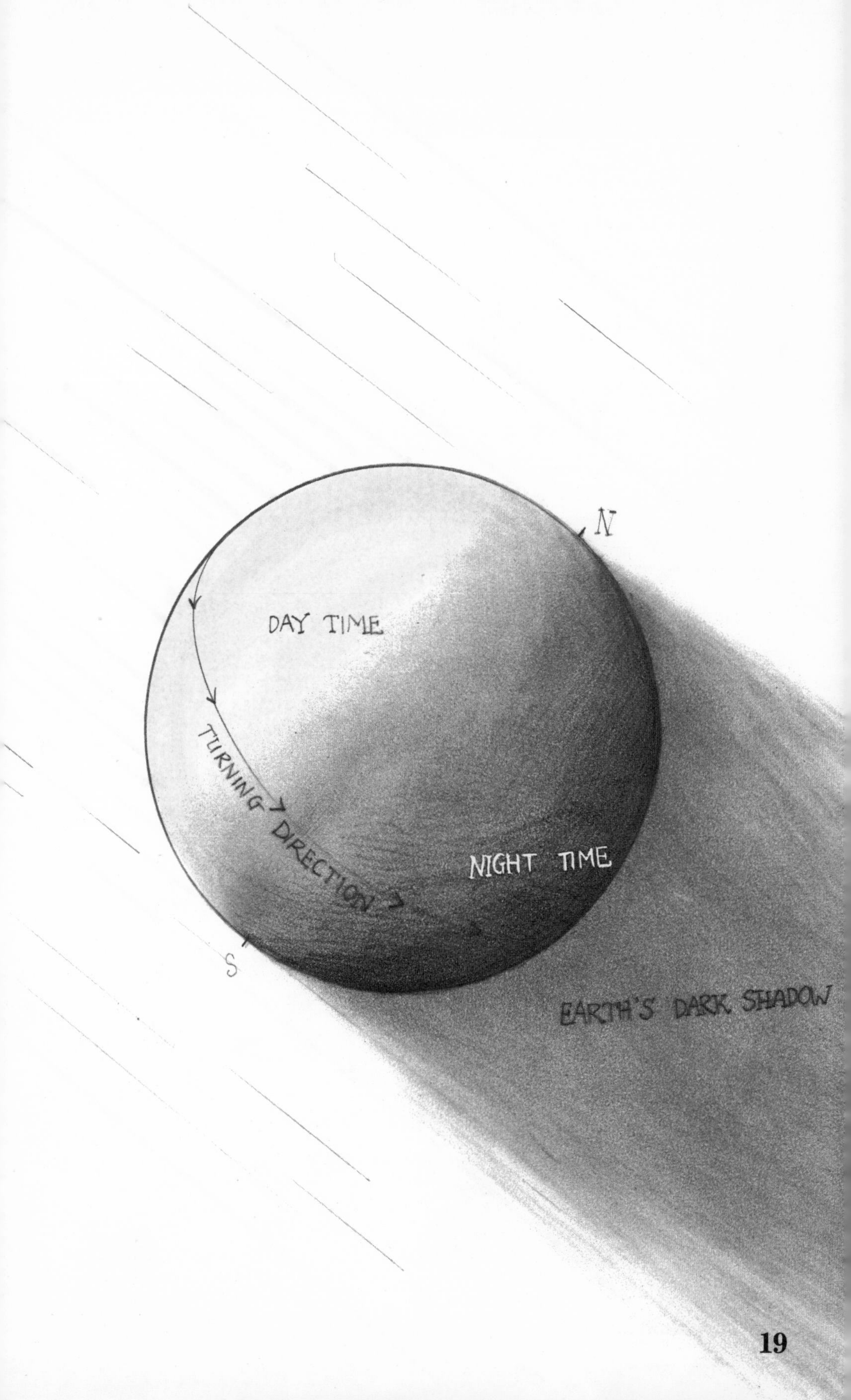

DAY TIME

N

TURNING DIRECTION

NIGHT TIME

S

EARTH'S DARK SHADOW

19

Shadows change in length
during the day.
When the sun rises in the morning,
shadows are very long.
Your shadow is much bigger
than you are at this time.
During the morning,
shadows get smaller and smaller.

Your shadow is smallest about noon.
In the afternoon,
shadows get larger and larger.
Shadows are very long at sunset.
Can you tell which of these pictures
is closer to noontime?

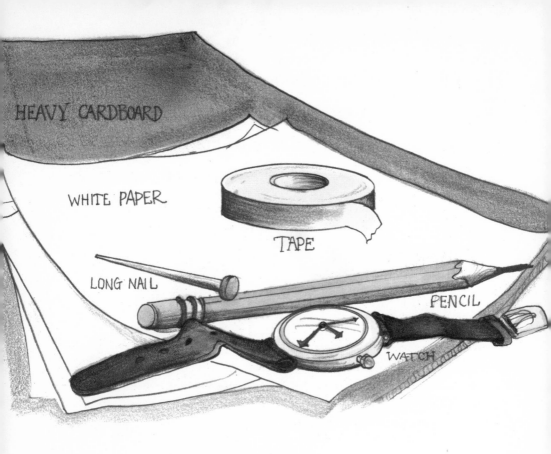

HEAVY CARDBOARD

WHITE PAPER

TAPE

LONG NAIL

PENCIL

WATCH

You can use shadows to help you tell time.
Here's how to make your own shadow clock.
You will need a piece of heavy cardboard,
a sheet of white paper, a long nail, some tape,
a pen or pencil, and a watch.
Tape the sheet of paper to the cardboard.
Stick the nail into the paper and cardboard
near one side.
Leave most of the nail showing.

Go outside and find a flat spot
of sunny ground where no one will bother you.
Place the cardboard on the ground.
Use a few small rocks to hold the cardboard
in place.

As soon after sunrise as possible,
start marking the shadow of the nail on the paper.
Mark the shadow every hour or so
until sunset.
Be sure to write the time next to each mark.
On the next day, check your shadow clock
to see if it tells you the right time.
Would your clock tell you the right time
if someone moved the cardboard?
If you move your shadow clock indoors,
be sure to make a mark on the ground where it was
so you can replace the clock in the same way.
Do you think your shadow clock
will be right on time a week later?
A month later?
All year long?
Try it and see.

People once used very accurate shadow clocks
to tell the time of day.
The clocks were called sundials.
The part of a sundial that casts a shadow
is called a gnomon (NO-mon).
The gnomon is at an angle to the clock.
The angle depends upon where the clock
is located on Earth.

But a sundial does not keep time
as do the clocks in your home.
One reason is that we sometimes set our clocks
an hour ahead, as when we have
daylight savings time.
Another reason is that some days,
according to sun time,
are longer or shorter than others.
But our clocks run at a steady speed
every day.
So sometimes our clocks are ahead of sun time,
and sometimes they are behind.

AD TIME HERE

GNOMON

I COUNT NONE BUT SUNNY HOURS

XI XII I II

X III

N

IX IIII

VIII W S E V

VII VI

29

You can make a magic shadow show
inside your house.
Wait until nighttime, or
draw all the shades in a room
so that it gets dark.
Tilt a lampshade so that the light
shines against a wall.

Hold your hand between the lamp and the wall.
First hold it one way, then another.
Does the shadow always
look like your hand?

Hold a toy truck or car in front of the lamp.
Does the shadow look like the truck?

Hold a doll, a telephone, a dish, and
this book in front of the lamp.
What do their shadows look like?

Shadows help you to know
what shapes things are.
Pictured here are shadows of
a ball and a piece of paper.
Which is the ball?
How do you know?

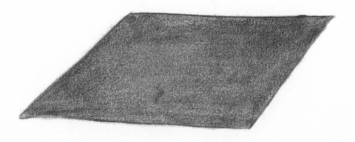

Can you always tell from the shape of a shadow
what is making the shadow?
Why do you think this is so?
Hold a ball or an orange in front of a light.
Turn it one way and another.
Does the shadow change shape?
Can you tell why or why not?

Again hold your hand between the lamp
and the wall.
Move your hand close to the lamp.
The shadow becomes large and not very dark.

Move your hand close to the wall.
The shadow becomes darker and smaller.
The closer you are to the light,
the larger and less dark is your shadow.

You can make shadows look like
other things too.
Put up two fingers and make a rabbit
wiggle its ears.

Hold your fingers sideways to make a duck quack.

Cross your hands and flap them
to see an eagle in flight.

Hold your fingertips together to make funny faces on the wall.

Make funny shadows and tell a funny story
to your friends.

Make scary shadows and tell a scary story.

Make big shadows.

Make little shadows.

Make lots of different shadows.

43

By now you should know a lot about shadows.
So here's a guessing game for you to try.
Can you match each thing with its shadow?

How many mistakes can you find in these drawings of shadows?

Can you guess what made these shadows?

Look all around you.
Shadows are everywhere.